THE ERA OF AI

Staying Human in a World of Machines

By

HAILEAB ZECHARIAS

DEDICATION

To my parents-teachers by calling, guides by spirit, whose love for learning shaped the soul of this work. Though you are no longer here in body, your wisdom lives in every word I write. And to every reader standing at the edge of a changing world: may this book remind you that you are still the source.

Author's Note

This book was not written to resist technology, nor to romanticize the past. It was written to pause. To pause long enough to remember that tools, no matter how advanced, gain meaning only from the hands and minds that guide them. Artificial intelligence can expand what we are capable of doing. It can accelerate creation, sharpen analysis, and widen possibilities. But it cannot choose what is worth building. That responsibility remains human. These pages are not a warning against progress. They are an invitation to awareness. An invitation to remain present as systems grow more powerful, to remain intentional as automation becomes effortless, and to remain responsible as choices scale beyond immediate sight.

I do not believe humanity is in opposition to this age. I believe we are its source. My hope is not that we compete with machines, but that we walk with them in purpose, using their power without surrendering conscience, welcoming innovation without forgetting meaning, and shaping the future with both intelligence and care.

This book does not offer instructions or predictions. It offers reflection. It asks questions that cannot be automated. It invites you to consider not only what technology makes possible, but what it asks of us in return. You are not late to this moment. You are not being replaced by it. You are still needed awake, thoughtful, and willing to choose with care. If these pages help you slow down, reflect, or see your role with greater clarity, then they have served their purpose. The future is not something happening to us. It is something we are participating in. And how we choose to participate still matters.

Table of Contents

INTRODUCTION

We are living through a moment that feels larger than history can easily contain. For centuries, tools extended the human hand. For decades, computers extended the human mind. Now, for the first time, machines appear to reflect intelligence itself. This shift has unsettled something deep within the modern world. People no longer ask only what technology can do; they ask what it means for them. If machines can write, analyze, create, predict, and respond, what, then, is left for the human being?

This book does not attempt to compete with artificial intelligence. It does not argue against progress, nor does it instill fear, evoke fantasy, or promote technological worship. Instead, it offers clarity. The defining question of our age is not whether machines will become powerful, they already have. The question is whether humans will remain conscious, disciplined, and responsible in a world where intelligence can be simulated but meaning cannot.

This is not a book about machines. It is a book about you: your agency in a world of automation, your identity in an age of replication, and your value in a time when speed is mistaken for wisdom and output is confused with purpose. Artificial intelligence can generate answers, but it cannot choose what matters. That responsibility still belongs to the human being. We are not entering the age of artificial intelligence alone. We are entering what I call the Mirror Age, an era in which technology reflects our thinking, our discipline, our values, and our emptiness with equal precision. What we see in that mirror will depend entirely on who we choose to become.

This book is written for those who refuse to disappear quietly into automation. For those who believe that progress without consciousness is not advancement. For those who understand that the future does not belong to the fastest systems, but to the most awake humans. You are not obsolete. You are still the source.

Chapter 1

You Are Still the Source

There is a quiet fear that many people no longer say out loud. It appears late at night, when the phone is face down, and the world grows still. When distractions fade, and the mind is left alone with itself. In those moments of silence, a question begins to surface. It feels simple, almost innocent, yet it carries unexpected weight. If machines can write, design, calculate, speak, and create, what is left for me? This fear does not belong to the careless or the unambitious. It does not arise from laziness, nor from resistance to change. It belongs to thoughtful, and disciplined people who invested years developing skills, cultivating knowledge, and shaping an identity around contribution and competence, with the expectation that this investment would matter.

The fear is not that artificial intelligence exists. Technology has always advanced, and humanity has always adapted. The fear is quieter than that. More personal. The fear is that you might become unnecessary. It feels new, but it is not. Every era of transformation has forced human beings to question their place in a changing world. What makes this moment different is not the presence of machines, but the nature of what they now appear to touch. Artificial intelligence does not merely extend physical labor or mechanical efficiency. It reaches into domains once considered uniquely human: language, reasoning, creativity, and decision-making. When tools begin to resemble thought, it is natural to question one's own relevance. Yet this question rests on a misunderstanding.

Human worth was never rooted in output alone. It was never defined solely by speed, precision, or productivity. Those were expressions of value, not its source. The source has always been something deeper, quieter, and less visible. You were never valuable because of how much you could produce. You were valuable because you could choose why to produce at all. Machines can generate results, but they do not generate intention. They can replicate patterns, but they do not define meaning. They can assist in creation, but they do not decide what deserves to be created. That distinction matters more now than ever before.

The rise of intelligent systems does not remove human significance. It exposes where that significance truly lives. As execution becomes easier, direction becomes more important. As answers become abundant, judgment becomes rare. As tools grow more capable, responsibility grows heavier, not lighter. What is left for you is not competition with machines. What is left is authorship. The ability to frame questions before answers are given. The courage to decide what matters when options multiply. The willingness to stand behind choices when consequences unfold.

Artificial intelligence may transform how work is done, how ideas are expressed, and how problems are solved. But it does not replace the human role of meaning-making. It does not feel consequence. It does not carry responsibility across time. It does not live inside the outcomes it helps produce, but you do.

The future will not be shaped by the most advanced systems alone, but by the quality of human consciousness behind them. Tools gain power from the hands that guide them. Intelligence gains direction from the values that frame it. You are not in opposition to this age, you are not late. You are not becoming irrelevant, you are still the source.

Chapter 2

The Mirror Age: Meeting Yourself Through AI

Every age has its defining invention. Fire gave us survival. The wheel gave us movement. The printing press gave us memory beyond the mind. Artificial intelligence gives us something unprecedented: a mirror that reflects our thinking to us.

For the first time in history, humanity has built a tool that does not merely extend the body or amplify physical power, but one that engages directly with thought itself. When you interact with an intelligent system, you are not simply using a machine. You are encountering a structured reflection of human knowledge: our language, assumptions, logic, priorities, and blind spots. Artificial intelligence does not reveal what it is. It reveals what humanity has encoded into it.

In this sense, we have entered what can be called the Mirror Age. An era in which technology no longer just serves us, but reflects us, sometimes with unsettling clarity. What appears intelligent on the surface is, at its core, a reassembly of what humanity has already expressed. Our questions, our values, our biases, and our errors are not erased by machines; they are returned to us in refined and accelerated form.

The danger, therefore, is not that machines will become human. The danger is that humans will stop recognizing themselves within what they build. As systems grow faster and more efficient, subtle shifts begin to occur in the human mind. When a system responds instantly, patience is quietly outsourced. When a system decides efficiently, deliberation begins to fade. When a system produces fluent language, reflection is replaced by acceptance. None of these changes happen dramatically. They occur gradually, almost politely, until habits form.

What begins as convenience slowly becomes dependence. The Mirror Age does not confront humanity with a hostile intelligence, but with its own reflection; magnified, accelerated, and stripped of context. The machine does not ask whether an answer is wise, only whether it is likely. It does not pause to consider meaning, only probability. Yet humans, exposed repeatedly to these outputs, may begin to internalize their rhythm. When answers arrive without effort, questions lose depth. When conclusions appear instantly, uncertainty feels unnecessary. When language is produced fluently, thought feels optional.

This is not because machines demand it, but because humans adapt. The mirror reveals not only intelligence, but intention. If a system optimizes for speed, it reflects a culture impatient with slowness. If it prioritizes efficiency, it mirrors a society uncomfortable with ambiguity. If it amplifies certain perspectives while neglecting others, it reflects collective choices about what was worth preserving and what was ignored.

Artificial intelligence does not create these imbalances. It exposes them. The Mirror Age forces a confrontation that previous technologies did not. Tools of the past changed what we could do. This tool changes how we think about doing. It challenges the relationship between effort and value, between knowledge and understanding, between information and wisdom. Human identity has always been shaped by resistance and by the limits of time, effort, and uncertainty. When those limits soften, identity must be re-examined. If intelligence is no longer scarce, what becomes precious? If answers are abundant, what gives questions their weight?

In the Mirror Age, the most important skill is not mastery of tools, but mastery of self. The ability to pause before accepting an output. The willingness to question not only whether something is correct, but whether it is appropriate. The courage to remain present when automation invites detachment. Machines reflect humanity faithfully. They do not distort on their own. What we see in them - clarity or confusion, depth or superficiality - originates with us. They amplify what we provide and return it at scale.

This is why the Mirror Age is not a technological crisis, but a human one. It asks whether we will use reflection to deepen understanding, or allow it to replace responsibility. Whether we will remain authors of meaning, or become passive consumers of generated coherence. To meet yourself through artificial intelligence is to face a choice. Not about machines, but about humanity's willingness to remain awake within its own creations. The mirror is already here. What it shows us depends on how honestly we are willing to look.

Chapter 3

The Myth of Artificial Intelligence

The fear that machines will replace human beings did not begin with artificial intelligence. It has surfaced repeatedly throughout history, whenever tools grew powerful enough to change how work, creation, or decision-making was done. What makes the current moment feel different is not the presence of fear, but the intimacy of the technology itself. These systems do not merely extend physical strength or mechanical output; they appear to touch thought, language, and creativity, the very traits people associate with identity. Because artificial intelligence can now write, design, calculate, and converse, it creates the impression that something essential is being taken over. Tasks that once required training, experience, and time can now be performed in seconds. For many, this raises a quiet but unsettling question: if machines can do what I do, where does that leave me?

This fear is understandable, but it rests on a misunderstanding of what is actually being replaced. What machines replicate is not human essence, but human process. They reproduce patterns, structures, and outputs derived from existing material. They do not originate meaning, intention, or direction. They operate within boundaries set by human choice, even when those boundaries are invisible to the user.

Replacement feels threatening because modern culture has trained people to equate their worth with productivity. We measure value by output, speed, and efficiency. When a system appears that can outperform humans on these metrics, it feels like a verdict on relevance. But this equation was flawed long before artificial intelligence arrived.

Human value was never rooted in execution alone. It was rooted in judgment, the ability to decide what should be done, why it should be done, and when it should not be done at all. Machines can execute tasks with remarkable precision, but they do not decide which tasks deserve to exist. They do not define goals; they optimize within them. The illusion of replacement emerges when execution is mistaken for authorship. When we see a machine produce text, images, or solutions, it is easy to assume it has replaced the role of the human creator. In reality, it has replaced only a portion of the labor, not the source of intention. The direction still originates outside the system.

Every meaningful human contribution begins before action. It begins with perception, with interpretation, with an understanding of context that cannot be reduced to data alone. These elements guide choices long before output is produced. Artificial intelligence enters the process later, operating on what has already been framed, requested, or allowed.

This distinction matters because fear grows in the absence of clarity. When people believe they are being replaced, they either resist technology blindly or surrender agency entirely. Neither response is necessary. Tools do not remove agency unless it is given away. They do not erase judgment unless judgment is neglected. History offers perspective here. When machines entered factories, people feared the end of work. Instead, the nature of work changed. When computers entered offices, people feared the end of expertise. Instead, expertise shifted toward interpretation, coordination, and decision-making. Each transition revealed the same pattern: tasks change, but responsibility remains human.

Artificial intelligence follows this same trajectory, even if its surface appears more personal. It handles complexity, scale, and repetition. What it does not handle is meaning. Meaning requires orientation toward values, consequences, and lived experience. It requires accountability across time. The belief that machines will replace humans entirely assumes that intelligence alone defines human worth. But intelligence divorced from responsibility is incomplete. A system can suggest actions without bearing the cost of those actions. A human cannot. This difference is not technical; it is moral.

What is being asked of people in this era is not competition with machines, but clarity of role. When execution becomes abundant, intention becomes scarce. When answers are easy to generate, questions become more important. The human role shifts toward framing problems, setting boundaries, and choosing directions worth pursuing.

The illusion of replacement fades when this shift is understood. Machines do not remove the need for human beings; they expose where human presence was always essential. They reveal that value was never in speed alone, but in discernment. Not in output alone, but in responsibility. You are not being replaced. You are being repositioned. The work is no longer only to do more, but to choose better. In a world filled with intelligent tools, the most irreplaceable skill is knowing what deserves to be done at all.

Chapter 4

What Machines Can Do, and What They Cannot

Machines can process vast amounts of information. They can absorb data from countless sources, recognize complex patterns, compare outcomes, and generate responses at a speed and scale no human mind can approach. This capacity allows them to perform tasks that once required teams of experts, long hours, and years of accumulated experience. In practical terms, these systems are extraordinarily capable, and their usefulness is undeniable.

Yet this ability, impressive as it appears, is only one dimension of intelligence. Information, no matter how abundant or well organized, does not become understanding by itself. Processing, even when flawless, does not transform into wisdom. Machines can describe the world with increasing accuracy, but description alone does not determine meaning, direction, or purpose.

A machine can tell us what exists and predict what is likely to happen next. It can calculate probabilities, rank options, and simulate outcomes. What it cannot do is decide what matters. It cannot determine which path is worth committing to, or which consequence is acceptable. These judgments do not emerge from data; they arise from values.

This is the quiet power machines do not have. They do not choose purpose. They do not feel the weight of consequence. They do not carry responsibility for the outcomes their outputs create in the world. A system can generate recommendations, but it does not stand behind them. It does not answer for the impact they have on lives, communities, or futures. In an age defined by rapid technological progress, capability is often mistaken for progress itself. Because something can be done faster, cheaper, or more efficiently, we assume it should be done. Because a process can be automated, we label it improvement without pausing to ask what might be lost in the transition. Speed becomes a substitute for direction, and optimization replaces reflection.

But speed without orientation leads nowhere. It only accelerates movement without ensuring that the destination is worth reaching. Human beings were never meant to be defined solely by how quickly they can produce results or how much information they can manage. They are defined by the values they uphold and the choices they are willing to stand behind, even when those choices are difficult or costly. Every major technological shift in history has raised the same underlying question: when our tools become more powerful, what remains distinctly human? Each time, the answer has been quieter than the fear surrounding it. What remains is judgment. What remains is conscience. What remains is the ability to say no when efficiency demands yes, and to choose restraint when acceleration is possible.

Artificial intelligence can simulate language, creativity, and even emotional tone with increasing sophistication. It can mirror human expression in ways that feel convincing and, at times, unsettling. Yet it does not experience regret. It does not feel moral tension. It does not bear responsibility for unintended consequences. It executes instructions; it does not carry accountability.

A human decision, once made, continues to echo forward. It shapes relationships, institutions, and future choices. A machine's output, by contrast, ends when execution is complete. Responsibility does not follow it into the future. This distinction is subtle, but it is fundamental.

For this reason, leadership is not replaced by intelligent systems; it is clarified by them. As machines take over execution, calculation, and repetition, human intention becomes more visible. When effort is reduced, meaning becomes the true measure of value. What we choose to build, support, or ignore reveals more about us than the tools we use to do it. The future will not belong to those who merely adopt the most advanced technologies first. It will belong to those who understand why they are using them and what they are willing to be responsible for. This requires a quiet discipline, a willingness to pause, to reflect, and to choose depth over constant acceleration.

This discipline is not resistance to technology. It is in alignment with humanity. It allows us to work with powerful tools without becoming shaped entirely by them. It reminds us that progress without purpose is not progress at all. You are not becoming irrelevant in an age of intelligent machines. You are being reminded of what cannot be replicated. The quiet power machines do not have is the power to choose meaning and to live with the consequences of that choice. That power has always belonged to you

Chapter 5

The Human Advantage in a Synthetic World

In a world increasingly shaped by machines, a quiet question moves beneath the surface of daily life: What can humans still do that technology cannot? As systems grow faster, more precise, and more capable, it becomes easy to believe that the human role is shrinking. But the opposite is true. What machines offer is power.

What humans offer is meaning. And meaning is the rarest force in any civilization. Artificial intelligence can calculate, optimize, generate, and predict. It can analyze vast amounts of data in moments and produce results that once required years of human effort. This is extraordinary. But none of it answers the most important question of all: What is worth doing? A machine can tell us what can be done. Only a human being can decide what should be done. This is the human advantage.

A system can propose thousands of solutions. Only a human can judge their consequences. An algorithm can execute instructions. Only a human can accept responsibility for the outcomes. A model can predict behavior. Only a human can choose integrity over efficiency. Human beings do not merely act; we answer for what we do. We carry the moral weight of choice. We feel the consequences of our decisions in the lives of others, and in the story, we tell ourselves about who we are becoming. This capacity for responsibility is not a weakness. It is the source of wisdom. Technology expands what is possible. But possibility alone does not create a future worth living in. Without judgment, power becomes reckless. Without conscience, efficiency becomes dangerous. Without meaning, progress becomes empty.

Machines operate within goals. Humans determine what those goals should be. Every system reflects the values of those who design it and the priorities of those who deploy it. If we optimize only for speed, we will create a fast world that forgets depth. If we optimize only for profit, we will build abundance without justice. If we optimize only for convenience, we will trade responsibility for comfort.

The more intelligent our machines become, the more essential human awareness becomes. The more automated our systems grow, the more necessary human responsibility becomes. This is not an age that diminishes humanity. It is an age that demands more of it. We were never meant to compete with machines. We were meant to guide them. To decide when to use them, when to restrain them, and when to refuse them. To ask not only Can this be done? but should it be done? To remember that what is technically possible is not always morally right.

The future will not belong to those who merely build the most powerful systems. It will belong to those who can hold power with conscience. In a synthetic world, the greatest advantage is not speed. It is wisdom. Not output, but purpose. Not automation, but responsibility.

Machines can extend our reach. Only humans can determine our direction. And as long as meaning must be chosen, as long as values must be lived, and as long as consequences must be owned, the human being will never be obsolete. This is your place in the age of intelligent machines. Not as a competitor. Not as a bystander. But as the source of judgment, purpose, and meaning. That is the human advantage.

Chapter 6

Discipline in the Age of Automation

Automation promises ease. It reduces friction. It shortens effort. It replaces repetition with speed. At first, this feels like freedom. But beneath the comfort of convenience, a quiet danger emerges: when effort disappears, so does the inner structure that effort once built. Discipline is not about control. It is about becoming. And in an age where machines increasingly remove the need to struggle, the human being must decide whether they will still choose the path that forms them.

What Discipline Really Is

Discipline is often misunderstood as rigidity, harshness, or denial. But at its core, discipline is not punishment. It is alignment. It is the ability to act in accordance with what matters, even when comfort, distraction, or automation offers an easier way out. A machine executes instructions. A human being chooses a direction. Discipline is not about doing more. It is about becoming someone who can be trusted with freedom.

When Convenience Replaces Character

In earlier eras, discipline was shaped by necessity. Survival required effort. Work demanded attention. Creation took time. But automation changes the environment. Today, answers are instant, labor is minimized, systems think ahead, and decisions are pre-filtered. The world becomes smoother, but the self becomes softer. Without resistance, will weaken. Without effort, identity dissolves. Without boundaries, intention fades. Convenience is not evil, but a life built only on ease rarely builds strength.

The Formation of the Inner World

Discipline does not exist for productivity alone. It exists for integrity. It forms patience, clarity, consistency, the ability to delay gratification, and the capacity to stay present when things are difficult. These qualities cannot be downloaded. They cannot be automated. They cannot be outsourced. They are formed only through repeated, conscious choice. A system may optimize behavior. Only a human can shape character.

The Quiet Power of Choosing Difficulty

In a world designed to make everything easier, choosing what is difficult becomes an act of sovereignty: to read deeply when summaries exist; to think slowly when answers are instant; to practice when shortcuts are available; to remain focused when distraction is engineered.

This is not nostalgia. It is preservation. Discipline is how the human being stays awake in a world that increasingly asks them to sleep.

Freedom Without Structure

Many believe automation will finally make humanity free. But freedom without structure does not liberate, it dissolves. When everything is effortless, nothing feels earned. When every desire is met instantly, nothing feels meaningful. When no discipline is required, nothing becomes sacred. True freedom is not the absence of limits. It is the presence of self-command. A disciplined mind does not obey impulses blindly. It chooses.

The Human Edge in a World That Thinks for You

AI can schedule your day. It can recommend your actions. It can anticipate your preferences. But it cannot decide who you are becoming. That question belongs only to you. Discipline is the bridge between potential and identity. It is what allows a human being to remain deliberate in a world that increasingly runs on automatic. You are not here to be optimized. You are here to be formed.

Becoming Someone in an Automated Age

The future will not be shaped only by technology. It will be shaped by the kinds of humans who live within it. Will they be comfortable but shallow, efficient but hollow, optimized but unanchored? Or will they be disciplined in thought, intentional in action, rooted in values no system can calculate? Automation will expand what is possible. Discipline will decide what is worthy.

Remaining Sovereign

In a world where machines increasingly manage tasks, the deepest human work becomes internal: remaining sovereign over one's attention, one's habits, and one's direction. Discipline is not resistance to technology. It is resistance to becoming less than oneself. And in the age of automation, this quiet resistance may be the greatest human strength of all.

Chapter 7

Attention: The Last Human Territory

In every era, there is something that determines who holds power. Once it was land, then industry, and then information. Now, in the age of intelligent systems, the true territory is attention. What you attend to shapes what you become. And what you allow to shape your attention slowly shapes your identity. In a world where machines are designed to capture, predict, and influence behavior, attention is no longer just a personal resource. It is a battlefield.

The Economy of Distraction

Modern systems are not built simply to inform you. They are built to hold you. Every notification, recommendation, and automated feed is optimized to maximize engagement, not meaning, not depth, not wisdom. Only time spent. The result is subtle but profound. Thought becomes fragmented. Presence becomes diluted. Reflection becomes rare. You are constantly stimulated, yet rarely centered. The danger is not that technology distracts you occasionally. The danger is that it trains you to live without stillness.

What Happens When Attention Is Outsourced

When machines choose what you see, what you read, and what you consider next, something essential is at risk: your inner direction. Attention is how values are formed. It is how beliefs are strengthened. It is how meaning is constructed. If your attention is guided primarily by algorithms, then your inner life slowly becomes shaped by priorities you did not choose, not by force, but by convenience.

Presence Versus Consumption

To be present is to inhabit the moment with awareness. To consume endlessly is to move through moments without ever arriving. Presence requires effort. Consumption requires only reaction. Machines are built for reaction. Humans are built for awareness. But awareness weakens when attention is constantly scattered. You begin to live at the surface of experience, always informed, rarely transformed.

Why Attention Is Sacred

What you give your attention to, you give your life to. Every hour absorbed in noise is an hour not spent in growth. Every moment of unconscious scrolling is a moment not spent in reflection, creation, or connection. This is not a moral judgment. It is an existential truth. Attention is the gateway through which identity is formed, purpose is discovered, and conscience is sharpened. Without deliberate attention, life becomes a series of reactions rather than a coherent direction.

Reclaiming the Inner Space

Reclaiming attention does not require rejecting technology. It requires governing your relationship to it by choosing what enters your mind, what deserves your time, and what shapes your emotional landscape. Silence becomes a discipline. Focus becomes an act of courage. Reflection becomes resistance, not against progress, but against fragmentation.

The Human Role in an Algorithmic World

AI can analyze behavior. It can predict preferences. It can optimize content. But it cannot decide what is worthy of your attention. That choice remains human. And in that choice lies your dignity. To attend deeply is to live deliberately. To live deliberately is to remain human.

Why Attention As Identity

You are not only what you believe. You are what you repeatedly focus on. Your thoughts shape your emotions. Your emotions shape your actions. Your actions shape your becoming. This is why attention is not a minor detail of modern life. It is the foundation of who you are becoming within it.

Why Choosing What You Serve

In a world competing endlessly for your attention, you must decide: will you serve noise or meaning, immediacy or depth, convenience or consciousness? The future will not only be built by what machines can do. It will be shaped by what humans choose to attend to. Because whatever commands your attention… commands your life.

Chapter 8

Creation Beyond Generation

The world is learning a new word: generate. Images are generated, text is generated, music is generated, Designs, ideas, and even voices are generated. And with this new power comes a quiet confusion: if machines can generate what once required human effort, what remains of creation? The answer is simple, but profound. Generation is not creation.

What Machines Actually Do

AI does not imagine. It does not desire. It does not struggle toward meaning. It analyzes patterns, recombines what already exists, and produces variations at scale. This is extraordinary. But it is not creative in the human sense. A system can generate a thousand versions of a painting style. Only a human can ask why the painting should exist at all. Generation produces output. Creation gives it purpose.

The Human Act of Origin

Creation begins before form. It begins with intuition, with a question, with a wound, with a vision, with a longing. These are not data points. They are experiences of being. A poem is not merely words arranged beautifully. It is a consciousness speaking from within life. A book is not merely structured information. It is a mind reaching another mind across time. Machines can arrange. Humans originate.

Why Meaning Cannot Be Automated

Meaning is not found in the object itself. It arises in the relationship between the creator, the creation, and the one who receives it. An algorithm can optimize a melody for popularity. But it cannot choose to write for grief, for love, for forgiveness, or for truth. It cannot suffer. It cannot hope. It cannot stand inside uncertainty and still choose expression. Creation is not just production. It is presence made visible.

The Illusion of Replacement

When people fear that AI will replace artists, writers, thinkers, and creators, they are really asking something deeper: if machines can make what I make, am I still needed? But what is being compared is not the same thing. A machine can generate a story, but only a human can tell one that must be told. A system can design a thousand logos. Only a human can decide what a symbol should stand for. Creation is not about novelty alone. It is about truth embodied in form.

Expression Versus Production

Modern culture increasingly confuses production with expression. More content. Faster output. Endless variations. But expression is rare because it requires vulnerability, consciousness, personal risk, and the courage to reveal what cannot be reduced to patterns. Creation is not about filling space. It is about revealing meaning. And meaning is born only in lived experience.

The Future of the Creator

In the age of AI, the human creator does not disappear. They become more essential. Not because machines fail, but because someone must decide what deserves to exist, choose the values embedded in what is created, and remain accountable for the impact of expression. The future does not need more outputs. It needs more intention.

Why Your Voice Still Matters

No system can speak from your life. No algorithm can feel what you have felt. No model can carry your history, your losses, your hopes, your becoming. Your voice is not valuable because it is unique in form. It is valuable because it is alive in meaning. Creation is the act of saying, "This matters to me," and offering that meaning to the world. Machines cannot do that. Only humans can.

The Future of the Creator

We do not create to compete with machines. We create to remember who we are. In a world where generation become infinite, creation becomes sacred. Not louder. Not faster. But truer. And in that truth, humanity does not vanish, it reveals itself.

Chapter 9

Identity in the Age of Imitation

We live in a time where almost anything can be copied. Voices can be cloned. Styles can be replicated. Thoughts can be remixed. Faces can be simulated. And with this ability comes a subtle, unsettling question: if everything can be imitated, what is truly mine?

The Difference Between Having a Form and Being a Self

AI can imitate your writing style, it can mimic your voice, it can reproduce your patterns of thought, but imitation is not identity. Identity is not how you sound. It is why you speak. It is not the shape of your work. It is the history, values, wounds, beliefs, and intentions that give that work meaning. A system may replicate form, but only a human carries a self.

Why Uniqueness Is Not Cosmetic

In the digital age, people are encouraged to "be unique" by changing aesthetics; different visuals, new styles, and personal branding. But uniqueness is not surface-level. True identity is formed through experience, struggle, choice, moral direction, and the stories that shaped you. No algorithm can live a life. No dataset can carry memory as meaning. Your identity is not what you look like to the world. It is who you are when no one is watching.

The Risk of Becoming Imitable

When identity is reduced to performance, it becomes reproducible. If who you are is only your productivity, your output, your aesthetic, or your public persona, then yes, machines can approximate you. But if who you are is your conscience, your compassion, your courage to choose what is right over what is easy, and your capacity to love, to suffer, to forgive, and to hope, then you remain irreplaceable.

The Inner Narrative

Identity is not something you display. It is something you live from. It is the story you tell yourself about what matters, what you stand for, and what kind of person you are becoming. Machines have no inner narrative. They do not ask, "Who am I?" They do not struggle with becoming. Identity requires consciousness. And consciousness is not a function.

Why Comparison Is the Enemy of Self

In a world of endless digital mirrors, it becomes easy to measure yourself against others on who is more successful, more visible, more efficient, more optimized. But identity does not grow through comparison. It grows through commitment. Commitment to your values, your discipline, your truth, and the kind of life you choose to build. No machine can choose a life. Only a human can.

Imitation Without Intention

AI can imitate behavior. But it cannot carry intention. It does not wake with purpose. It does not fear betrayal of self. It does not protect meaning. Identity is not simply how you act. It is why you act when no rule forces you to. That "why" cannot be trained.

Becoming Instead of Performing

The future will reward performance. But fulfillment will come only from becoming. You are not here to be a better copy. You are here to be a truer self. Not louder. Not more visible. But more aligned. When you live from identity rather than imitation, your life cannot be replaced because it is not a pattern. It is a presence.

What Remains Yours

Your conscience. Your choices. Your responsibility. Your capacity to love. Your willingness to stand alone when truth demands it. These are not features. They are the essence of being human. And in an age where imitation becomes effortless, authentic identity becomes sacred.

Chapter 10

Purpose in a Programmable World

The more powerful technology becomes, the more one question quietly returns: what is all of this for? We build faster systems. We automate entire industries. We optimize decisions, production, communication, and even creativity. But progress without direction is not destiny. It is motion without meaning. And in a world increasingly shaped by programmable intelligence, the human being must face the most ancient question of all: why am I here?

When Capability Outpaces Meaning

Never before has humanity been able to do so much with so little effort. Tasks that once required years now take seconds. Information that once demanded libraries now fits in a pocket. Solutions appear instantly. Yet many feel more uncertain, more disconnected, more directionless than ever. Because capability does not answer purpose. Power does not define value. You can build anything. But what is worth building?

The Silent Crisis of Direction

Technology gives answers faster than we can ask questions. It solves problems before we have decided which problems matter. This creates a subtle crisis: we know how to do things, but not always why we should.

When purpose is unclear, efficiency becomes hollow. Life becomes productive, but not meaningful. A programmable world can give you outcomes. Only a conscious human can give those outcomes significance.

Purpose Is Not a Function

Machines operate by function. Humans live by meaning. A system can optimize a route. It cannot decide where a life should go. Purpose is not found in speed, success, visibility, or automation. It is found in what you choose to stand for, who you choose to serve, and what kind of future you decide is worth contributing to. Purpose is not something you calculate. It is something you commit to.

Why Choice Still Defines You

In a world where systems increasingly suggest what to do next, the human being risks forgetting the power of choice. Not the choice between options, but the choice of direction. Choice is what transforms action into meaning. Two people can perform the same task. While one person does it for convenience, the other person does it in service of a value. The action may look identical. The purpose makes them worlds apart.

The Temptation of Optimization

Optimization is seductive. It promises better outcomes with less effort. But when life becomes only about optimization, something essential is lost: the question of what deserves to exist. A machine can tell you how to be more efficient. It cannot tell you what is worthy of your life. Purpose is not about maximum output. It is about alignment with what matters. Living as a Source of Meaning

To live with purpose in a programmable world is to remain a source rather than a function. Not simply reacting to systems. Not merely following recommendations. But choosing to shape your life according to values no algorithm can compute. This does not require grand gestures. It begins in quiet decisions: what you devote your time to, what you refuse to become, and what you protect even when it is inconvenient. Purpose is built one choice at a time.

When Progress Needs a Compass

Technology will continue to advance. That is inevitable. But without a human purpose, progress becomes directionless power. History shows us this clearly: power without meaning does not liberate, it disorients. The future will not be saved by smarter systems alone. It will be shaped by humans who remember why anything matters at all.

Choosing a Life That Means Something

You are not here merely to function. You are here to become. To decide what kind of person you will be, what kind of work deserves your energy, and what kind of world you are willing to help build. In a programmable world, the deepest human act is not efficiency. It is purpose, and purpose begins when you stop asking only what can be done and start asking what is worth doing.

Chapter 11

Responsibility in the Age of Intelligence

As intelligence becomes embedded in systems, tools, and decisions, a quiet shift occurs. Power increases, while accountability becomes harder to see. When outcomes are produced by algorithms, predictions, and automated processes, the question is no longer simply what happened. It becomes: who is responsible? And in that question lies one of the most important moral challenges of our time.

Power Without a Face

In earlier eras, power had a human face, a leader decided, and a builder designed. A writer persuaded, while a teacher shaped minds. But in the age of intelligent systems, influence is often invisible. A recommendation changes a life, a model denies an opportunity, and an automated decision determines access, risk, or direction. There is no voice, no eyes, no human presence, but only outcome. And when power becomes faceless, responsibility begins to dissolve.

Why Intelligence Does Not Equal Accountability

AI can analyze situations. It can predict probabilities. It can recommend actions, but it cannot stand behind a consequence. Responsibility is not a function of intelligence. It is a moral position. To be responsible is to say, "This decision came through me. I accept its weight." A system cannot do that. Only a human can.

The Danger of Moral Outsourcing

As systems grow more capable, there is a temptation to outsource judgment. Phrases like "the data said so," "the algorithm recommended it," or "the system made the decision" sound neutral, but they hide a dangerous shift: the relocation of responsibility from conscience to code. When humans stop owning decisions, power becomes unanchored. And unanchored power has never ended well. Responsibility as the Core of Humanity What makes a human being human is not simply thought. It is the ability to answer for one's actions. To recognize harm, impact, consequence, and the weight of choice. Responsibility is what transforms intelligence into ethics. Without it, knowledge becomes cold, capability becomes indifferent, and progress becomes morally blind.

Living in a World of Delegated Decisions

Today, systems increasingly decide what you see, what you are offered, what is prioritized, and what is filtered out. This can feel convenient. But it also creates distance between action and accountability. When something goes wrong, who answers? The developer? The company? The user? The model? Responsibility becomes diluted across layers of abstraction. And when responsibility is everywhere, it is often nowhere.

The Human Role: To Remain Answerable

In an age of intelligence, the deepest human role is not to compete with machines. It is to remain answerable. To ask: is this right? Who is affected? What are the consequences? Am I willing to stand behind this? No system can ask these questions for itself. Only a human can.

Ethics Is Not an Upgrade

Many believe ethics can be programmed. But ethics is not a set of rules. It is a lived responsibility. Rules can guide behavior. But responsibility requires conscience. A system can be compliant. Only a human can be accountable. This is why no amount of intelligence can replace moral agency.

Choosing to Carry the Weight

Responsibility is heavy. It slows decisions, complicates progress, and demands reflection. But it is also what keeps power human. To be responsible in the age of AI is to refuse the comfort of moral distance. It is to say, "Even if a system assisted, the choice is still mine." That is not weakness, it is dignity.

The Future Needs Accountable Humans

Technology will continue to evolve. Systems will grow more capable. Decisions will become faster and more complex. But the future will not be judged by how intelligent our machines became. It will be judged by how responsibly humans used them. Responsibility is not a limitation on progress. It is the conscience that makes progress worth having. And in a world of intelligent systems, the most human act of all remains simple: to stay accountable for what we choose to do.

Chapter 12

Relationships in a Digital Reality

Technology connects the world. But connection is not the same as communion. We can message across continents, share thoughts instantly, and maintain hundreds of contacts without ever truly meeting another soul. And in this new digital closeness, a deeper question quietly emerges: are we becoming more connected, or more alone?

The Difference Between Contact and Encounter

A message is not a meeting. A reaction is not a response. A presence on a screen is not the same as a presence in a room. Digital systems make interaction effortless. But meaning is not created by ease. It is created by attention, vulnerability, and time. Machines enable contact. Only humans create encounter.

The Subtle Erosion of Depth

When communication becomes constant, it often becomes thin. Short messages replace long conversations. Reactions replace reflection. Visibility replaces understanding. We speak more, but reveal less. We are always reachable, yet rarely met. The danger is not technology itself. It is the slow replacement of depth with speed.

Why Human Presence Cannot Be Simulated

AI can generate language. It can imitate empathy. It can respond with warmth and structure. But it cannot feel the silence between words, sense the emotion behind a glance, or hold the unspoken weight of another person's story. Presence is not what is said. It is what is shared. A human relationship is not an exchange of data. It is a meeting of inner worlds.

The Temptation of Safe Distance

Digital interaction offers control. You can edit what you say, curate what you show, and withdraw without confrontation. This feels safe. But safety can become isolation. Real relationships require risk, patience, misunderstanding, forgiveness, and the willingness to be seen imperfectly. No algorithm can carry these tensions. They belong to life.

Loneliness in a Connected World

We live in the most connected era in history. And yet, many experience a quiet loneliness that technology cannot soothe. Because loneliness is not the absence of people. It is the absence of being known. You can be followed by thousands and still feel unseen. You can be surrounded by messages and still feel unheard. Only presence, true presence, breaks loneliness.

Why Relationship Is the Core of Meaning

We do not find meaning in isolation. We find it in relation. In being recognized, understood, challenged, and cared for. Human beings are not designed merely to function. We are designed to belong. No machine can belong. No system can love. No algorithm can share life.

Choosing Depth in a Digital World

To remain human in a digital reality is to choose conversation over noise, presence over performance, listening over reacting, and depth over reach. This does not mean rejecting technology. It means refusing to let it replace what is sacred. Your time, your attention, and your presence are not resources to be optimized. They are gifts to be given.

The Future of Human Connection

Technology will continue to evolve. Virtual spaces will become more immersive. Simulated companionship will grow more convincing. But no system will ever replace the warmth of being truly understood, the courage of being vulnerable, or the dignity of being chosen by another human being. The future may be digital. But meaning will remain relational.

Remaining Human Together

In a world of screens and systems, the most radical act may be simple: to sit with another person, to listen without distraction, to speak without performance, and to remain when leaving would be easier. Relationships are not a feature of life. They are its foundation. And in the age of AI, the deepest truth still stands: we do not become human alone. We become human together.

Chapter 13

Work, Worth, and the Redefinition of Value

For centuries, human worth has been closely tied to work: what you do, how productive you are, and what you contribute. But as machines increasingly perform tasks once reserved for human hands and minds, a quiet tension emerges: if my work can be automated, what does that say about my value?

When Productivity Is No Longer the Measure

AI can write. It can calculate. It can design. It can analyze. Tasks that once required years of training can now be completed in moments. This is a triumph of technology. But it also challenges an identity many people have lived inside: the belief that "I am what I produce."

When production becomes effortless for machines, humans are forced to ask a deeper question: who am I beyond my output?

The Mistake of Equating Worth with Utility

Modern society often treats people as units of usefulness. How efficient are you? How much do you contribute? How replaceable are you? But usefulness is not the same as value. A tool is useful. A person is meaningful. Your worth does not come from what you generate. It comes from who you are, what you stand for, and how you live in relation to others. Machines can be useful. Only humans can be significant.

The Quiet Fear Beneath Automation.

Beneath debates about job displacement lies a more personal anxiety: if my role disappears, do I disappear with it? This fear is not economic alone. It is existential. We have been taught to measure ourselves by productivity, achievement, and visibility. When those metrics are threatened, identity itself feels fragile. But your life was never meant to be justified by output. You were not born to be a function. You were born to be a presence.

Work as Expression, Not Identity

Work can be meaningful. It can be creative. It can be a form of service and self-expression. But work is not who you are. When identity collapses into occupation, any change in circumstance becomes a crisis of self. Automation exposes this fragility and invites a redefinition: work is something you do, worth is something you are.

What Machines Cannot Replace

AI can perform tasks. But it cannot care for meaning, hold responsibility, act from conscience, choose purpose over convenience, or love another person as a moral commitment. These are not skills. They are dimensions of being human. No amount of automation touches the deepest layers of what makes a life matter.

The New Measure of Value

In a world where efficiency is increasingly automated, value will not belong to those who merely produce faster. It will belong to those who think ethically, act responsibly, relate deeply, create meaning rather than content, and choose purpose over performance. The question will not be: how much can you do? It will be: who are you becoming?

Dignity Beyond Function

History shows that when people are reduced to their function, something essential is lost. A human being is not a role, a job title, or a line of output. You matter not because of what you provide to a system, but because you are a conscious, relational, responsible being in the world. Your dignity is intrinsic. It does not need to be earned.

Work in the Age of Meaning

As machines take over more tasks, human work will not disappear. But it will be redefined, not as survival alone, not as identity, but as an expression of values.

The most meaningful work of the future may not be what pays the most or scales the fastest, but what heals, teaches, guides, protects, and gives form to what is human.

Remembering Who You Are

You are not your output. You are not your productivity. You are not your efficiency. You are a being who can choose meaning, hold responsibility, love, create, forgive, and hope. In an age where machines redefine what can be done, humans must remember who they are. Not producers first. Not functions in a system. But sources of meaning in a world that desperately needs it.

Chapter 14

Mortality, Meaning, and the Limits of Intelligence

No matter how advanced technology becomes, there is one reality it cannot erase: we are finite. We age. We suffer. We lose. We die. And it is precisely this finitude that gives human life its depth. In an age where machines grow more capable each day, a profound contrast emerges. Intelligence may scale endlessly, but meaning is born from limitation.

Why Finitude Gives Life Weight

If life were endless, urgency would disappear. If choices had no finality, they would lose significance. If time were infinite, moments would become interchangeable. It is because life is fragile that it is precious. It is because time is limited that it is meaningful. A system can process forever. A human must choose what matters now. Mortality is not a defect of life. It is the condition that gives life its gravity.

The Illusion of Technological Transcendence

Modern culture often flirts with the idea that technology might one day overcome human limits, extending life indefinitely, digitizing consciousness, and preserving identity through data. These ideas are not merely scientific. They are philosophical. They ask whether we can escape being human. But what would be lost if we did? If fear of death vanished, would courage still exist? If suffering disappeared, would compassion still matter? If loss were impossible, would love still carry its depth? To remove finitude is not to perfect life, it is to empty it of meaning.

Why Intelligence Alone Cannot Carry Meaning.

Intelligence solves problems. It does not answer existence. A machine can calculate probabilities. It cannot ask, "What does my life mean?" It can simulate language about death, purpose, and love. But it cannot stand inside these realities. Meaning arises not from processing, but from being, from knowing that this moment will not return, from understanding that every choice echoes into a limited future, from carrying the awareness that life is both beautiful and fragile.

Suffering as a Source of Depth

No one seeks suffering. But it is often through suffering that meaning is discovered. Loss teaches what truly matters. Pain reveals what cannot be replaced. Mortality clarifies priorities. A system avoids suffering by design. A human transforms it into wisdom. This is not romanticizing pain. It is recognizing that what hurts us also shapes us. Without vulnerability, life would be efficient, but it would not be human.

The Question Machines Will Never Ask

AI will grow in capability. It may one day simulate conversation about death, love, faith, and purpose. But it will never ask, "What should I do with my life?" Because it does not have a life. That question belongs only to beings who know they will not last forever. And it is that question (quiet, personal, unavoidable) that gives human existence its depth.

Living in the Shadow of Time

To live meaningfully is not to deny mortality. It is to honor it. It is to choose what deserves your time, who deserves your presence, and what is worth building, even knowing it will one day pass. Finitude does not diminish life. It intensifies it. Every moment becomes a gift. Every relationship becomes sacred. Every decision becomes a statement of what you believe matters.

Why Humanity Cannot Be Reduced to Data

Data can record a life. It cannot contain one. You are not your history of actions. You are the consciousness that lived them. You are the one who felt joy, regret, love, fear, and hope, not as information, but as existence. No archive can store that. No model can replicate it.

Choosing Meaning in a Finite World

In the face of intelligent machines and endless automation, the deepest human task remains unchanged: to choose a life that means something. Not the longest life. Not the most optimized life. But a life aligned with what you believe is true, good, and worthy. Mortality does not make life smaller. It makes it serious. And in that seriousness lies the dignity of being human.

The Quiet Triumph of Being Human

Machines may one day outperform us in almost every measurable way. But they will never face their own end, love in the presence of loss, or choose meaning knowing time is short. And because of this, humanity does not become obsolete in a technological future. It becomes essential, not because we are stronger. Not because we are faster, but because we are finite, and therefore capable of meaning.

Chapter 15

The Future Is a Choice

The future is often spoken of as if it were inevitable, as if technology advances on its own and systems determine outcomes while history simply happens to us. But the future is not a machine. It is a human decision, repeated every day.

Beyond Technological Destiny

There is a popular myth that progress has a direction of its own, which means that whatever can be built will be built, whatever can be automated will be automated, and whatever can be optimized will be optimized. But technology does not move by itself. It is created, deployed, and shaped by human values. Every system reflects the priorities of those who design it. Every algorithm carries assumptions. Every innovation expresses a philosophy, whether acknowledged or not. The future is not what machines will do. It is what we choose to do with them.

Power Without Direction Is Not Progress

We are entering an era of extraordinary capability. We can automate knowledge, simulate creativity, scale influence instantly, and shape environments digitally. But capability alone does not define progress. A faster world is not necessarily a better one. A more efficient society is not automatically a more humane one. The question is not how powerful our systems will become. It is what kind of world we are trying to build.

Values Are the Architecture of Tomorrow

Every civilization is built on invisible foundations: what it honors, what it protects, what it is willing to sacrifice, and what it refuses to become. These are not technical decisions. They are moral ones. If a society values only efficiency, it will become cold. If it values only convenience, it will become shallow. If it values only control, it will become inhuman. Technology amplifies values. It does not create them.

Choosing Humanity Over Optimization

The greatest danger of the AI age is not that machines will surpass us. It is that we may begin to measure ourselves by machine standards: speed over depth, output over meaning, performance over integrity. What makes a future worth living in is not how optimized it is. It is how human it remains. A humane future values dignity over efficiency, wisdom over acceleration, relationship over reach, and conscience over convenience. These values do not appear automatically; they must be chosen.

The Responsibility of This Generation

Every generation inherits tools it did not create and must decide how to use them. Ours has inherited unprecedented power. We can shape minds through information, influence behavior through systems, and redesign work, communication, and even identity itself. With such power comes an ancient responsibility: to ensure that what we build serves life, not replaces it. The future will not be defined by what was possible. It will be judged by what was chosen.

You Are Not a Passenger in History

It is tempting to feel small in the face of global systems, to believe that decisions are made elsewhere and that individuals do not matter. But history is not shaped by tools. It is shaped by choices made by human beings, sometimes quietly, sometimes courageously, often without recognition. You shape the future in what you support, what you resist, what you normalize, and what you refuse to accept. You are not a bystander to progress. You are a participant in its direction.

What Kind of World Do You Want to Leave?

One day, this era will be looked back upon. People will ask whether intelligence was used to deepen wisdom, whether automation freed humanity or emptied it, and whether systems were built to serve life, or lives were built to serve systems. These questions will not be answered by machines. They will be answered by the values we lived by.

The Courage to Choose Deliberately

Choosing a future is not about grand declarations. It is about daily alignment, choosing to act with conscience when speed is easier, to value people when efficiency is rewarded, and to protect what is human when optimization is praised. These choices rarely make headlines. But they shape everything.

Becoming the Architects of Meaning

Technology will continue to evolve. Systems will grow more powerful. Possibilities will expand. But meaning will not be generated by machines. Meaning will come from what we decide to honor, what we choose to build, and what we refuse to trade away for convenience. The future is not something that happens to us. It is something we become. And what we become will depend on one enduring truth: the future is a choice.

Chapter 16

The Responsibility of Being Human

There is a quiet question waiting at the edge of every technological revolution. Not what can we build next? Not how far can this go? But something deeper, something that lingers beneath progress itself:

Who are we becoming?

This question does not announce itself during moments of excitement or discovery. It does not appear when new tools first arrive, when innovation feels magical, or when possibilities seem endless. It waits patiently. It emerges only after the novelty fades, after artificial intelligence shifts from marvel to infrastructure, from experiment to expectation.

When the noise of innovation settles, what remains is not the machine. What remains is the human being standing before it, unchanged in essence, yet newly challenged in responsibility. We often speak about the future as though it belongs to technology, as though progress itself were an independent force moving beyond human hands. But the future has never belonged to tools. It has always belonged to those who decide how tools are used, guided, limited, and restrained. Artificial intelligence will write faster. It will analyze deeper. It will simulate creativity. But it cannot choose why. That choice has always belonged to the human being, and it still does.

Beyond Capability

Human value has never been defined solely by what we are capable of producing. It has been defined by what we decide is worth producing, protecting, and passing forward. History does not remember humanity only for its inventions. It remembers us for the meaning we attached to them. Fire could warm a home or destroy a city. The printing press could educate or manipulate. Electricity could illuminate or dominate.

The internet could connect or divide. The tool itself never chose the outcome. Humanity did. Artificial intelligence follows the same pattern. It does not arrive with values embedded. It magnifies whatever it is placed in service of. When placed in service of speed without reflection, it accelerates emptiness. When placed in service of power without conscience, it amplifies harm. When placed in service of efficiency without care, it erodes presence. But when placed in service of wisdom, integrity, and human dignity, it becomes something rare; a mirror through which humanity can better understand itself rather than disappear within its own creations. Technology reveals us, it does not replace us.

The Signature Only You Carry

Every human life leaves a mark. Not always visible. Not always celebrated. But always real. Your voice. Your perspective. Your discipline. Your conscience. Your compassion. These are not features that can be engineered or replicated at scale. No system can replicate the weight of a decision made with awareness. No algorithm can feel the gravity of choosing what is right when what is easy is readily available. No machine can carry regret, responsibility, faith, love, or moral consequence. These are not technical attributes. They are human signatures. And in a world where output becomes increasingly automated, meaning becomes increasingly rare. What remains human begins to matter more, not less. Presence becomes valuable. Intention becomes powerful. Choice becomes defining.

Mastery Without Surrender

To live wisely in the age of artificial intelligence is neither to reject it nor to worship it. It is to master it without surrendering oneself. Use AI to think faster, but not to think for you. Use it to explore more, but not to determine your values. Use it to amplify your work, but never to replace responsibility for what that work becomes. The danger is not that machines will become intelligent. The danger is that humans will drift away from intention. Humanity is not protected by competition with machines. It is preserved through clarity, awareness, and conscious choice. Progress does not require the abandonment of depth. Efficiency does not demand the loss of meaning. To become more human, not less, is the quiet discipline of this era.

The Quiet Future

The future will not arrive with spectacle or ceremony. It will not announce itself as a single moment of transformation. It will enter quietly into classrooms, hospitals, studios, workplaces, homes, and private moments where a single human being must decide: Do I act with awareness, or do I outsource judgment? Do I choose depth, or do I accept convenience? Do I remain present, or do I allow automation to decide for me? The age of artificial intelligence will not be judged by what machines were capable of achieving. It will be remembered by what humans chose to become while using them.

A Continuing Responsibility

Human beings were never created to be replaced. They were created to be responsible for thought, responsible for direction, and responsible for meaning. Technology may shape the structures of the world. But only humanity shapes what the world stands for. This responsibility does not place you outside progress, but within it. Not as a spectator. Not as a passive user. But as a conscious participant, one who carries something no system ever will: a conscience, a will, and a sense of purpose. This is not a closing moment. It is a point of orientation. Machines can generate. But only humans decide what is worth creating. And that decision continues forward, beyond this chapter, beyond this moment, quietly shaping what comes next. What follows is no longer about understanding systems from a distance. It is about living inside them with awareness. Insight becomes incomplete if it remains theoretical. What matters now is how intelligence (human and artificial) meets daily life, shapes habits, influences attention, and quietly rewrites the way choices are made. Wisdom in this era is not dramatic. It does not announce itself through resistance or fear. It appears in small, repeated acts of presence. In the willingness to pause. In the courage to choose depth when speed is available. In the discipline to remain conscious while powerful tools operate silently in the background.

The age unfolding ahead does not ask humanity to withdraw. It asks humanity to participate with clarity. To move forward without surrendering inner authority. To engage progress while remaining rooted in meaning. This is where responsibility becomes lived, not discussed.

From here on, the focus shifts from what technology can do to how a human being chooses to live while using it. Not as a reaction to change, but as an author within it. What emerges next is not fear of the future, but a way of inhabiting it with intention. This is where thought turns into practice.

Chapter 17

Conscious Living in a Synthetic World

The world shaped by intelligent systems does not arrive all at once. It enters quietly into routines, habits, interfaces, and decisions so small they barely register. A recommendation here. An automation there. A subtle shift in how attention is guided, how work is organized, and how choices are framed.

Life in a synthetic world is not defined by machines replacing humans. It is defined by machines surrounding human life so completely that awareness becomes the deciding factor. What changes is not only what we do, but how easily we stop noticing why we do it. Conscious living, in this context, is not resistance. It is not nostalgia, it is presence, and it is the discipline of remaining awake inside systems designed for efficiency, speed, and convenience. Technology simplifies actions. Consciousness preserves intention.

The challenge of this era is not complexity, but ease. When decisions are anticipated, optimized, and suggested before they are fully formed, it becomes tempting to drift. To allow systems to carry the weight of choice. To trade authorship for comfort. Yet a life guided entirely by convenience slowly loses depth.

Conscious living begins with a simple shift: reclaiming awareness in ordinary moments. Choosing to notice how tools shape behavior. Asking whether efficiency serves meaning, or quietly replaces it. Pausing long enough to sense whether a decision aligns with values rather than momentum. In a synthetic world, attention becomes the most human act.

Every system competes for focus. Notifications fragment thought. Algorithms reward reaction. Speed becomes a measure of worth. But human awareness was never designed for constant acceleration. It was designed for discernment, the ability to slow, to integrate, and to understand before acting.

To live consciously is to protect that inner tempo. This does not mean abandoning technology. It means refusing to let technology determine the rhythm of one's inner life. It means using tools deliberately rather than habitually. It means remembering that convenience is not neutral; it shapes perception, expectation, and patience. Work, too, transforms in a synthetic world. Tasks become automated. Processes abstracted. Output measured with increasing precision. Yet meaning does not scale the same way productivity does. A human being still seeks purpose, contribution, and dignity in effort. Conscious work asks different questions than efficient work. It asks not only what can be done faster, but what is worth doing well? It asks not only what can be delegated, but what should remain personal?

There are dimensions of work; judgment, care, and responsibility that cannot be automated without cost. When these are surrendered entirely, something essential erodes, even if performance improves. The same is true in learning, creativity, and relationships. Synthetic systems can assist, suggest, and enhance. But they cannot replace the lived experience of struggle, curiosity, and growth. They cannot substitute the depth that comes from effort chosen freely rather than optimized externally.

Conscious living requires boundaries with intentional limits, not rigid walls. Choosing when to engage and when to step back. Deciding which tools serve growth and which quietly dull it. Recognizing that not every available enhancement is necessary, and not every shortcut is wise. This is not a call for purity. It is a call for balance.

A synthetic world amplifies whatever is left unattended. When awareness fades, systems decide. When attention fragments, meaning thins. But when consciousness remains present, technology becomes a partner rather than a director. The most important skill of this era is not technical mastery alone, but inner orientation. Knowing who you are before systems begin to suggest who you should be. Remembering values before metrics begin to define success. Choosing depth before speed becomes the only language spoken.

Conscious living does not ask for perfection. It asks for a return. Again and again, returning to intention. Returning to presence. Returning to the quiet authority of choosing rather than drifting. In a world that increasingly thinks for us, awareness becomes an act of authorship. And authorship; over attention, over values, over direction, is what allows humanity to live meaningfully inside the systems it creates, rather than disappear into them.

Chapter 18

The Ethics That Cannot Be Automated

As intelligent systems grow more capable, a quiet assumption often follows: that what can be optimized can also be entrusted. That what performs well can be allowed to decide. That efficiency, once proven, deserves authority. But ethics do not emerge from performance. They emerge from responsibility. Artificial intelligence can process information at extraordinary scale. It can detect patterns, predict outcomes, and recommend actions with impressive accuracy. Yet none of these abilities constitute moral judgment. They do not answer the question of what should be done, but only what could be done.

Ethics begins where capability ends.

Moral judgment is not the result of calculation alone. It is shaped by context, by values, by lived experience, and by an awareness of consequence that extends beyond metrics. It requires the ability to weigh competing goods, to accept uncertainty, and to remain accountable when outcomes are imperfect. No system carries that burden. Algorithms can be trained on historical data, but history itself is not moral guidance. It reflects past choices, past power structures, past blind spots. When systems inherit these patterns without reflection, they reproduce harm with greater efficiency, not greater wisdom.

Automation does not eliminate bias. It accelerates it when left unchecked. This is why ethics cannot be delegated. They must be practiced. In medicine, a system may recommend a treatment, but it does not sit with a patient in uncertainty. In law, an algorithm may assess risk, but it does not live with the consequences of a judgment. In governance, systems may model outcomes, but they do not answer to the human cost of decisions made at scale. Responsibility cannot be outsourced without erosion. Ethical judgment requires more than accuracy. It requires care. It requires restraint. It requires the willingness to pause when speed is available, but reflection is necessary. These qualities are not inefficiencies. They are safeguards.

The temptation of automation lies in its clarity. Systems provide answers without hesitation. They offer confidence without doubt. But moral life is rarely that clean. It unfolds in ambiguity, where values conflict, and outcomes remain uncertain. To live ethically in an automated age is to resist the desire for false certainty.

This does not mean rejecting intelligent systems. It means placing them in proper relation to human judgment. Tools should inform decisions, not replace them. Recommendations should support responsibility, not dissolve it. The danger is not that machines will make decisions. The danger is that humans will stop owning them.

Ethics requires ownership.

It requires the courage to say, this decision is mine, even when guided by data. It requires the humility to recognize that no model captures the full weight of a human life. It requires the discipline to intervene when automation drifts away from dignity. These responsibilities do not diminish as systems improve. They intensify. As intelligence becomes easier to deploy, wisdom becomes harder to cultivate. As systems grow faster, ethical reflection must grow steadier. The future does not demand fewer moral agents. It demands more conscious ones.

What cannot be automated is the willingness to be accountable. To accept responsibility not only for outcomes, but for the values that shaped them. To stand behind choices when consequences unfold slowly, imperfectly, and without applause. To remain answerable to something deeper than performance.

Ethics, at its core, is not a set of rules. It is a posture. A way of standing in the world with awareness of impact and care for what lies beyond immediate gain. In an age of intelligent machines, this posture becomes the clearest expression of humanity. Not because machines are dangerous, but because power without responsibility always is.

Chapter 19

Creativity, Meaning, and the Inner Life

As machines learn to generate images, music, language, and ideas, a subtle confusion begins to surface. If creativity can be simulated, if style can be replicated, if expression can be produced on demand, then what distinguishes human creation from output?

The answer does not lie in novelty alone. It lies in meaning. Creativity has never been defined only by the act of making. It has been defined by the inner life from which making emerges. Human creation is shaped by memory, longing, struggle, curiosity, and care. It carries the imprint of lived experience of questions asked without certainty, of choices made without guarantee.

Machines can produce form. They do not live the life behind it. When a system generates a poem, it does not ache. When it composes music, it does not remember. When it paints an image, it does not risk itself in expression. The output may resemble creativity, but resemblance is not equivalence.

Meaning does not arise from arrangement alone. It arises from intention. The inner life, which is the quiet space where reflection, doubt, imagination, and conscience reside, cannot be automated. It cannot be optimized. It cannot be accelerated without cost. It unfolds at a human pace, shaped by attention and depth rather than speed. In a world that rewards instant production, the inner life becomes easy to neglect. When creation is effortless, reflection may seem unnecessary. When output is abundant, meaning may appear optional. Yet it is precisely here that something essential is at risk. Without inner engagement, creativity thins.

Human creativity has always been an act of translation, bringing something unseen into form. It draws from questions that do not have immediate answers. It carries vulnerability. It exposes perspective. It invites others not only to observe, but to feel, to consider, to recognize themselves. This is why creative work matters even when machines can imitate it. Not because humans are faster or better at production, but because humans create from within consequence.

A human being lives inside what they make. Ideas shape identity. Words shape thought. Art shapes memory. Creation is not separate from the creator; it feeds back into the inner world, influencing how one understands self and others. Machines do not experience this feedback They do not grow through expression. They do not change because of what they produce.

The presence of artificial creativity invites a choice. Either human beings retreat from the inner life, allowing surface-level production to dominate, or they deepen their engagement with meaning, using tools to assist expression without replacing reflection. The danger is not imitation. The danger is substitution.

When meaning is replaced by efficiency, when expression is valued only for reach rather than resonance, the inner life begins to flatten. Creativity becomes content. Expression becomes output. The human voice becomes interchangeable. Yet meaning resists this reduction. Meaning emerges when a human being pauses long enough to ask not only Can this be made, but why should it be? It appears when attention is sustained, when curiosity is allowed to wander, when silence is given space to speak. The inner life requires protection in an age of constant generation.

This protection does not demand isolation from technology. It demands intention within it. Choosing when to use tools and when to sit with uncertainty. Allowing questions to mature before answers are produced. Remembering that not every idea must be expressed immediately, and not every expression must be optimized.

Creativity thrives where patience exists. Meaning deepens where effort is chosen freely rather than removed entirely. When struggle disappears too quickly, insight often follows it. When friction vanishes, understanding may never fully form. To remain human in a world of synthetic creativity is to stay connected to the inner sources of expression. To value depth over speed. To treat creation not as performance, but as participation in something larger than oneself. Machines may help us create more, but only humans decide what creation is for. And that decision, rooted in the inner life, is where meaning continues to live, even as the world around it becomes increasingly automated.

Chapter 20

Power, Restraint, and the Future We Choose

Power has always arrived before wisdom. Every transformative tool in human history expanded capacity faster than understanding. Fire came before restraint. Industry came before ethics. Digital connection came before discernment. Artificial intelligence follows the same pattern, not as an exception, but as a continuation. What makes this moment decisive is not the scale of power alone, but the speed at which it spreads. Intelligent systems extend influence far beyond individual intention. Decisions propagate instantly. Errors multiply quietly. Consequences unfold at a distance from those who initiated them. Power becomes diffuse, abstracted, and difficult to trace back to human choice.

In such conditions, restraint becomes a form of intelligence. Restraint is often misunderstood as limitation. In truth, it is orientation. It is the capacity to pause in the presence of possibility. To recognize that not every capability must be exercised, and not every advancement must be deployed without question.

Power without restraint does not simply create risk. It creates blindness. When systems can do more than we fully comprehend, the temptation is to trust capability over judgment. To assume that scale implies legitimacy. To confuse what works with what is wise. Yet history repeatedly shows that the most damaging outcomes emerge not from malicious intent, but from unexamined momentum.

The future is shaped less by what we can build than by what we choose to limit. Restraint introduces space for reflection. It allows values to catch up with innovation. It creates room for ethical deliberation before consequences harden into reality. Without restraint, power moves faster than responsibility, and the cost is paid later, often by those least involved in the decision. This is not an argument against progress. It is an argument for maturity.

Maturity recognizes that power amplifies both wisdom and error. It understands that intelligence divorced from care becomes brittle. That speed untampered by reflection leads to outcomes that cannot be easily undone. The most meaningful choices of the future will not be made only by engineers or systems. They will be made by individuals and institutions willing to ask not only What is possible? but What is appropriate? Not only what can be optimized, but what should be preserved?

Restraint requires courage. It requires the willingness to delay, to reconsider, to say no when incentives reward yes. It requires standing against the momentum of inevitability and remembering that the future is not a force to submit to, but a direction to be chosen. Artificial intelligence magnifies human intention. When intention is unclear, restraint becomes the safeguard. When values are unexamined, restraint becomes the boundary. When power grows faster than understanding, restraint becomes responsibility.

The future will not be decided by the most advanced tools alone. It will be shaped by the presence or absence of restraint in those who guide them. To choose restraint is not to fear power. It is to respect it. The world ahead will remember not only what humanity built, but how carefully it chose to build it. Whether it recognized that the highest form of intelligence is not unlimited expansion, but the wisdom to stop, reflect, and choose with care. In an age of unprecedented power, restraint is not weakness. It is the clearest expression of strength.

Chapter 21

Becoming the Source Again

At a certain point, every era of acceleration forces a return. Not backward, but inward. When systems grow complex and power expands beyond easy comprehension, the question is no longer how far technology can go, but where responsibility must rest. That place has always been the human being.

For much of modern history, progress has encouraged distance from consequence, from labor, from the outcomes of decisions made at scale. Automation increases that distance. Abstraction widens it. When systems act on our behalf, it becomes easier to forget that agency has not disappeared. It has only been redistributed.

To become the source again is to reclaim authorship. Authorship does not mean control over every outcome. It means ownership of direction. It means recognizing that tools extend intention, but do not replace it. That systems execute, but do not originate purpose. That power, however advanced, still answers to the values that guide it.

In an age of intelligent machines, it is tempting to surrender authorship gradually. To allow recommendations to become decisions. To let efficiency stand in for judgment. To mistake delegation for wisdom. This surrender is rarely dramatic. It happens quietly, through convenience, through habit, through trust unexamined.

Yet authorship fades not because it is taken, but because it is neglected. Becoming the source again begins with awareness. Awareness of where choices are made. Of how decisions are framed. Of which values are being reinforced through repetition. It requires noticing when one's role shifts from participant to observer, from decision-maker to confirmer of what systems propose.

The human capacity to choose does not vanish when tools improve. It becomes easier to overlook. To reclaim that capacity is not to resist technology, but to situate it. To remember that tools exist to serve human purposes, not to define them. To reassert that meaning is not an output, but a responsibility carried by those who decide what is worth pursuing. Responsibility, in this sense, is not burden alone. It is dignity.

It affirms that human beings are not interchangeable nodes in a system, but sources of intention, conscience, and care. That they remain accountable not only for what is done efficiently, but for what is done thoughtfully. That progress does not absolve judgment, it demands it. Becoming the source again also requires humility. The humility to admit uncertainty. To acknowledge limits. To accept that not every question has a clean answer, and not every solution should be automated.

It asks for patience in a culture that rewards immediacy, and reflection in a world optimized for speed.

This humility is not weakness. It is the posture that allows wisdom to form. When humans remain the source, systems become extensions rather than replacements. Technology amplifies insight rather than eroding it. Power is guided rather than unleashed. Progress becomes directional rather than automatic.

The future does not require humans to be faster than machines. It requires them to be clearer than machines. Clear about values. Clear about responsibility. Clear about what must remain human even as capabilities expand. To become the source again is to remember that authorship is not a privilege granted by technology. It is a condition of being human. And in a world increasingly shaped by what we build, the quiet decision to remain the source; to choose with awareness, to guide with care, to stand behind what unfolds becomes one of the most consequential acts of all.

Chapter 22

What Remains Human

There comes a moment in every age when progress pauses long enough for us to look at ourselves. Not because innovation slows, but because something within us asks a quieter question, one that cannot be answered by speed or scale. What are we becoming as everything around us accelerates? This book has not argued against intelligence, nor has it asked you to retreat from the future. It has walked beside you through a changing landscape and reminded you of something essential: tools do not define direction. They magnify it. They carry forward the values, intentions, and awareness of those who create and guide them.

Artificial intelligence can analyze, predict, optimize, and replicate. It can mirror language, simulate creativity, and extend human reach. But it does not wake with uncertainty. It does not wrestle with meaning. It does not feel the weight of choice or the quiet pull of conscience. Those burdens and those gifts remain human. What remains human is not efficiency, but presence. Not speed, but awareness. Not output, but responsibility.

In a world increasingly shaped by automation, the human capacity to pause becomes an act of courage. To reflect before acting. To choose depth over noise. To remain attentive when distraction is rewarded. These are not outdated traits. They are stabilizing forces in an unstable age.

The future will not be shaped by advanced systems alone. It will be shaped by the quality of judgment behind them. Intelligence without wisdom scales mistakes. Automation without ethics amplifies harm. Progress without reflection becomes directionless. This is why humanity is not being replaced, it is being tested. The test is not technical. It is moral.

Will we remain awake as our tools grow more capable? Will we stay accountable as delegation becomes effortless? Will we protect meaning when replication becomes cheap?

To remain human in this era does not require rejection of technology. It requires authorship. It asks that we remain the source of values, of direction, of restraint, of care. It asks that we remember that every system inherits the inner posture of its creators. You do not need to compete with machines, you do not need to outrun them, and you do not need to prove your worth through speed or scale.

Your worth is already present in your capacity to choose with awareness. The age ahead will belong to those who integrate power with humility, intelligence with compassion, innovation with restraint. To those who understand that progress is not measured only by what we can build, but by what we refuse to lose. What remains human is the ability to ask why before asking how. What remains human is the courage to slow down in order to see clearly. What remains human is the responsibility to guide what we create rather than surrender to it.

As you step forward into this unfolding future, remember this: You are not late. You are not obsolete. You are not outmatched. You are early to a deeper responsibility. And that responsibility to choose wisely, to act consciously, and to remain human is the most advanced intelligence of all.

AUTHOR'S NOTE

This book was not written to resist technology, nor to romanticize the past. It was written to remind us of something simple and enduring: tools gain meaning only from the hands that guide them. Artificial intelligence can expand what we can do.

It can sharpen thought, accelerate creation, and widen possibilities. But it cannot choose what is worth building. That responsibility remains human. My hope is not that we compete with machines, but that we walk with them in purpose, using their power without surrendering our conscience, welcoming progress without forgetting meaning, and shaping the future with both intelligence and care. You are not in opposition to this age. You are its source.

www.ingramcontent.com/pod-product-compliance
Lightning Source LLC
LaVergne TN
LVHW100327210926
848480LV00003B/1282